Portable Art

A Project
by Celia Forner

Hauser & Wirth Publishers

Foreword

Marc Payot & Sara Harrison

We are thrilled to be able to present 'Portable Art: A Project by Celia Forner', an artistic pursuit that has been almost ten years in the making. A passionate and informed art collector with depth of knowledge and appreciation for jewelry, Celia has realized her wonderful vision in an exhibition of her own design, contextualizing precious wearable creations with a selection of artworks.

Celia began the project in 2008, working with Louise Bourgeois to conceive a stunning series of gold and rhodium cuffs. Since then, she has collaborated with a total of 15 artists from around the world to create incredible pieces all completed with a dedication to a high level of craftsmanship and an exacting attention to a wide range of precious materials.

Continuing on from the tradition of artists creating jewelry, Celia has pushed her scope to engage with the idea of wearability, blurring the boundaries between jewelry and sculpture, uniting artists' visions with the capabilities of craftsmanship. The final pieces were documented in an energetic and playful photo shoot directed by Celia, with photography by Gorka Postigo and modeling by Rossy de Palma — the images capture the essence of the project.

We are very proud of this collaboration with Celia and all the artists involved; the result, seen in the pages that follow, is a truly unique and inventive exhibition that celebrates an expanded vision of creativity.

LIFE
LIFE

FEBRUARY 11 · 1966 · 35¢

John Baldessari

14

Phyllida Barlow

30

Louise Bourgeois

36

Stefan Brüggemann

48

Subodh Gupta

54

Mary Heilmann

62

Andy Hope 1930

68

Cristina Iglesias

74

Matthew Day Jackson

80

Bharti Kher

86

Nate Lowman

92

Paul McCarthy

96

Caro Niederer

102

Michele Oka Doner

108

Pipilotti Rist

114

Rossy de Palma
photographed by Gorka Postigo

John Baldessari

Mr. Blue Bird on my Shoulder (with Diamonds), 2013
Bird: enameled silver, diamonds. Shoulder stand: metal, suede

Mr. Blue Bird on my Shoulder (with Rubies), 2013
Bird: enameled silver, rubies. Shoulder stand: metal, suede

Mr. Blue Bird on my Shoulder (with Sapphires), 2013
Bird: enameled silver, sapphires. Shoulder stand: metal, suede

Previous spread: Crowd Arm (Gold on Gold), 2016 (left)
Spike: 22 kt yellow gold plated silver
Elbow: 22 kt yellow gold plated silver and silver

Crowd Arm (Gold on Silver), 2016 (right)
Spike: 22 kt yellow gold plated silver
Elbow: 22 kt yellow gold plated silver and silver

Crowd Arm (Gold on Silver), 2016
Spike: 22 kt yellow gold plated silver
Elbow: 22 kt yellow gold plated silver and silver

Nose Earring (Silver), 2017
Silver

Nose Earring (Gold), 2016
18 kt yellow gold

Nose Earring (Silver), 2017
Silver

Picture Frame for the Face Necklace
(Yellow Gold), 2011 (left)
22 kt yellow gold plated silver, convex series

Picture Frame for the Face Necklace
(Rose Gold), 2011 (middle)
Rose gold plated silver, flat series

Picture Frame for the Face Necklace
(Rhodium), 2012 (right)
Rhodium plated silver, concave series

Picture Frame for the Face Necklace
(Rose Gold), 2011
Rose gold plated silver, concave series

Picture Frame for the Face Necklace
(Rhodium), 2011
Rhodium plated silver, flat series

Phyllida Barlow

untitled: brooch III, 2015-2016
Electroformed, silver plated and hand-painted
with enamel

untitled: brooch II, 2015-2016
Electroformed, silver plated and hand-painted
with enamel

untitled: brooch I, 2015-2016
Electroformed, silver plated and hand-painted
with enamel

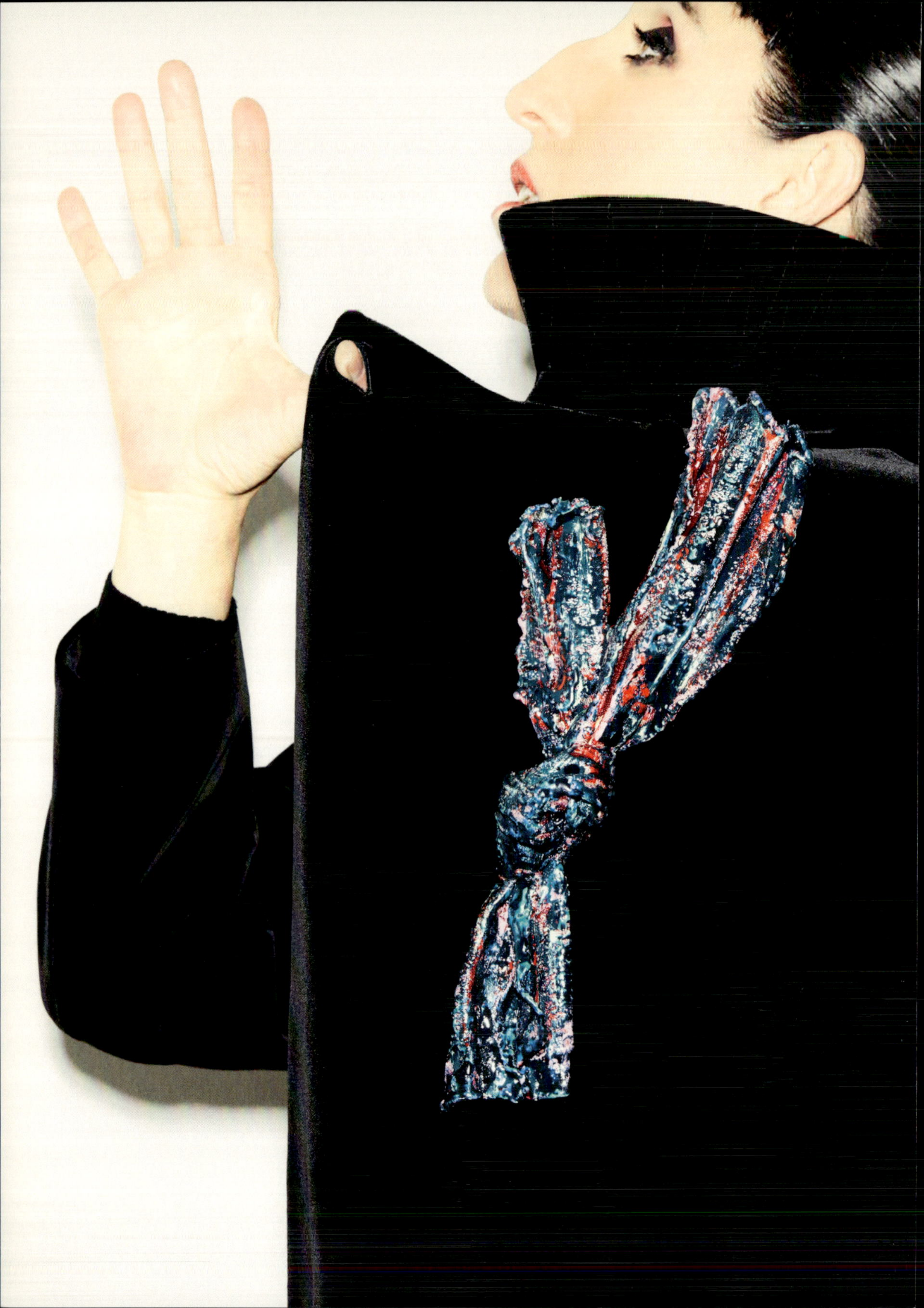

Jewelry is a hybrid form—part sculpture, part decoration, part craft, part virtuosic skill, part decadence, part expedience —maybe all style and no content? Anything can be jewelry just as anything can be art.

Phyllida Barlow

untitled: brooch I, 2015-2016
Electroformed, silver plated and hand-painted with enamel

Louise Bourgeois

Spiral, 2008 (top)
Rose gold plated silver

Cuff, 2008 (left)
Rhodium plated silver

Cuff, 2008 (right)
22 kt yellow gold plated silver

The spiral is an attempt at controlling the chaos. It has two directions. Where do you place yourself, at the periphery or at the vortex? Beginning at the outside is the fear of losing control; winding in is a tightening, a retreating, a compacting to the point of disappearance. Beginning at the center is affirmation, the move outward is a representation of giving up control; of trust, positive energy, of life itself.

Louise Bourgeois

Cuff, 2008
Rhodium plated silver

Cuff, 2008
Rose gold plated silver

Spiral, 2008
22 kt yellow gold plated silver

Following spread: Spiral, 2008 (left)
22 kt yellow gold plated silver

Spiral, 2008 (right)
Rhodium plated silver

Previous spread: Spiral, 2008
Rose gold plated silver

Spiral, 2008
Rhodium plated silver

Cuff, 2008
22 kt yellow gold plated silver
on pink marble stand

Stefan Brüggemann

Fool's Gold, 2016
Cube: pyrite
Ring: pyrite and 18 kt yellow gold

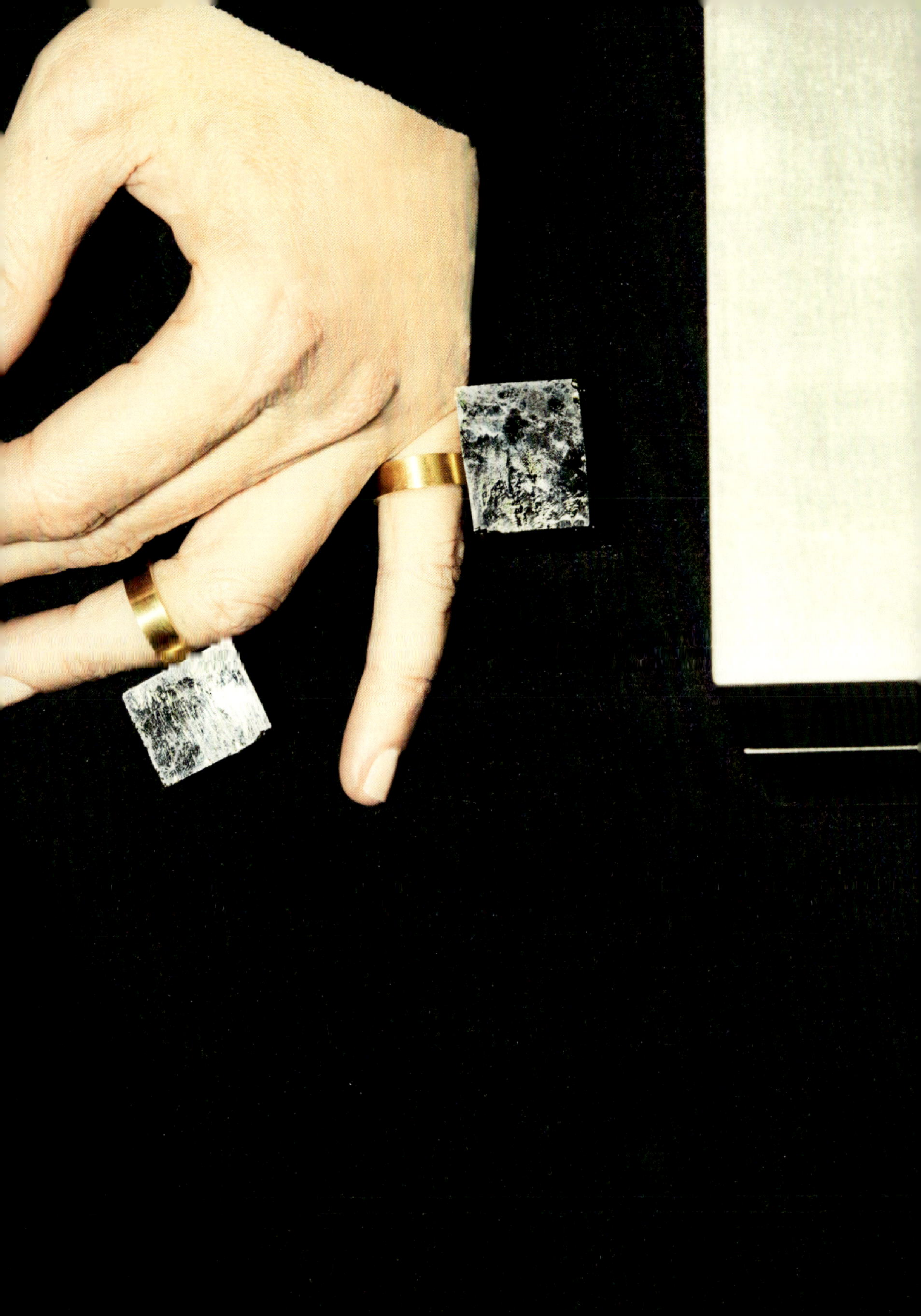

Fool's Gold, 2016
Cube: pyrite
Ring: pyrite and 18 kt yellow gold

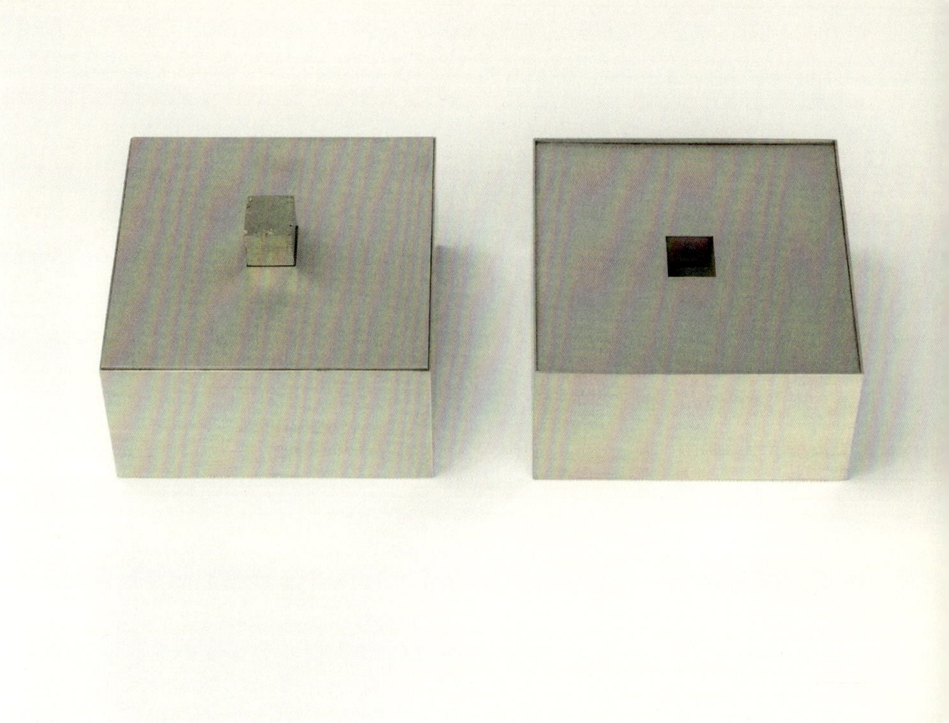

Fool's Gold, 2016
Cube: pyrite
Ring: pyrite and 18 kt yellow gold

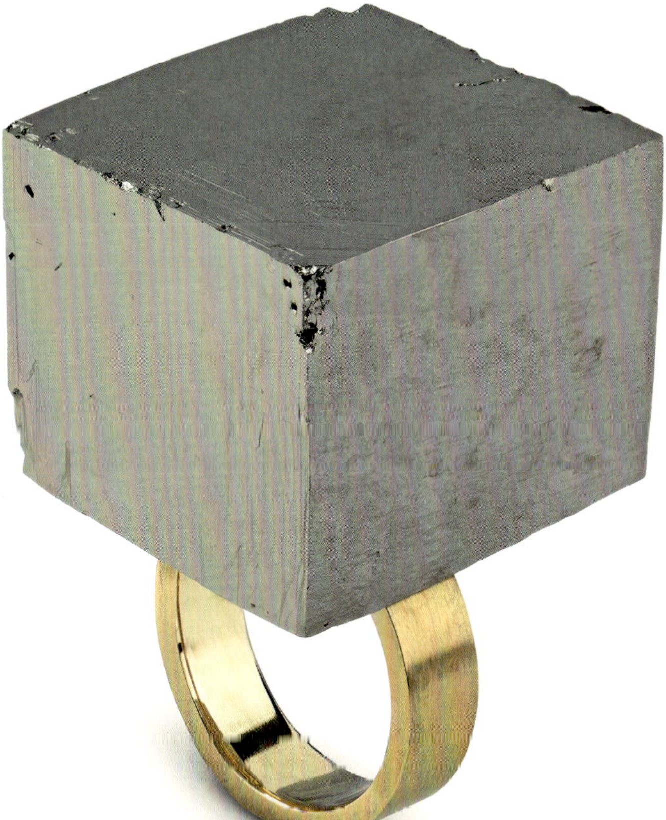

Subodh Gupta

Untitled, 2013
Pendant: 18 kt yellow gold and emeralds
Chain: 18 kt yellow gold

Untitled, 2012 (detail)
Pendant: 18 kt yellow gold and colored diamonds
Chain: 18 kt yellow gold

When someone is looking at a sculpture, the gallery or museum or whatever space the sculpture is in provides a lot of the context for the sculpture and influences the viewer's perspective. However, when someone is wearing an artwork, his or her own body and persona becomes the context for the work, so it can entirely change the meaning of a work. In some sense, a certain amount of control that one may have had over an artwork, as an artist, is lost; you have to hand that over to the person wearing the work.

Subodh Gupta

Untitled, 2012
Pendant: 18 kt yellow gold and colored diamonds
Chain: 18 kt yellow gold

Untitled, 2008
Pendant: silver, ruby and brilliant-cut
colorless and black diamonds
Chain: silver

Mary Heilmann

Untitled, 2016
3 hollow silver disks, lacquered
Chain: silver with matte finish

Untitled, 2016 (left)
5 hollow silver disks, lacquered
Chain: silver with matte finish

Untitled, 2016
3 hollow silver disks, lacquered
Chain: silver with matte finish

My life with jewelry began with
opening my mother's
'jewelry box' in San Francisco
when I was a little girl.
Holding the diamond bracelets
and rings, putting them
on, looking in the mirror to see
how several pieces
glittered together at once.

There were several generations of
rings, necklaces, brooches,
bracelets in there: Grandmothers
and even great grandmothers
from far away: Italy, Germany,
Ireland, and even Queens,
New York.

Mary Heilmann

Untitled, 2016
4 hollow silver disks, lacquered
Chain: silver with matte finish

Andy Hope 1930

Aztek, 2017
18 kt yellow gold

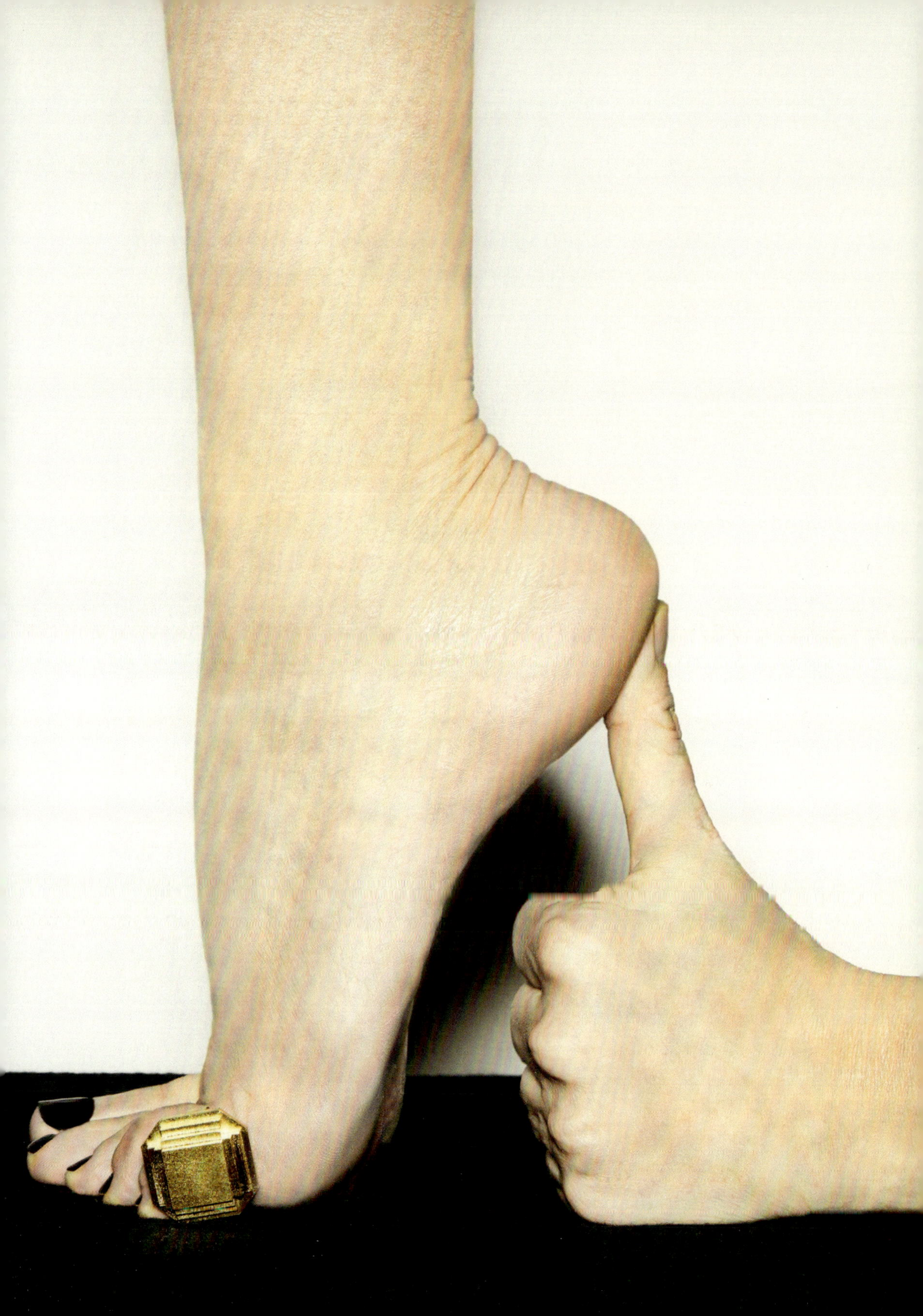

MACHINE

TIME

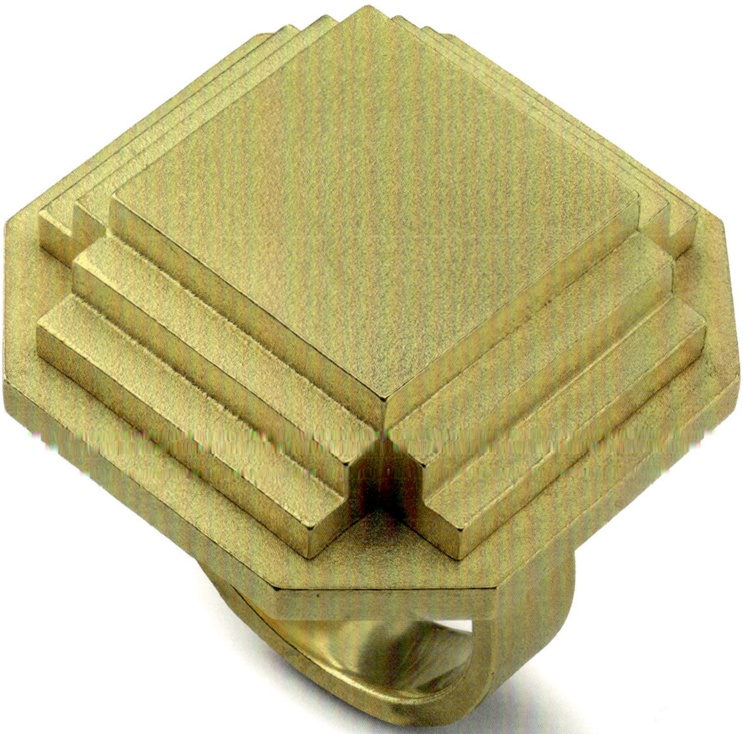

Time Machine, 2017 (left)
18 kt yellow gold and iron

Aztek, 2017
18 kt yellow gold

Whistleblower, 2017
18 kt yellow gold

Whistleblower, 2017
18 kt yellow gold

Cristina Iglesias

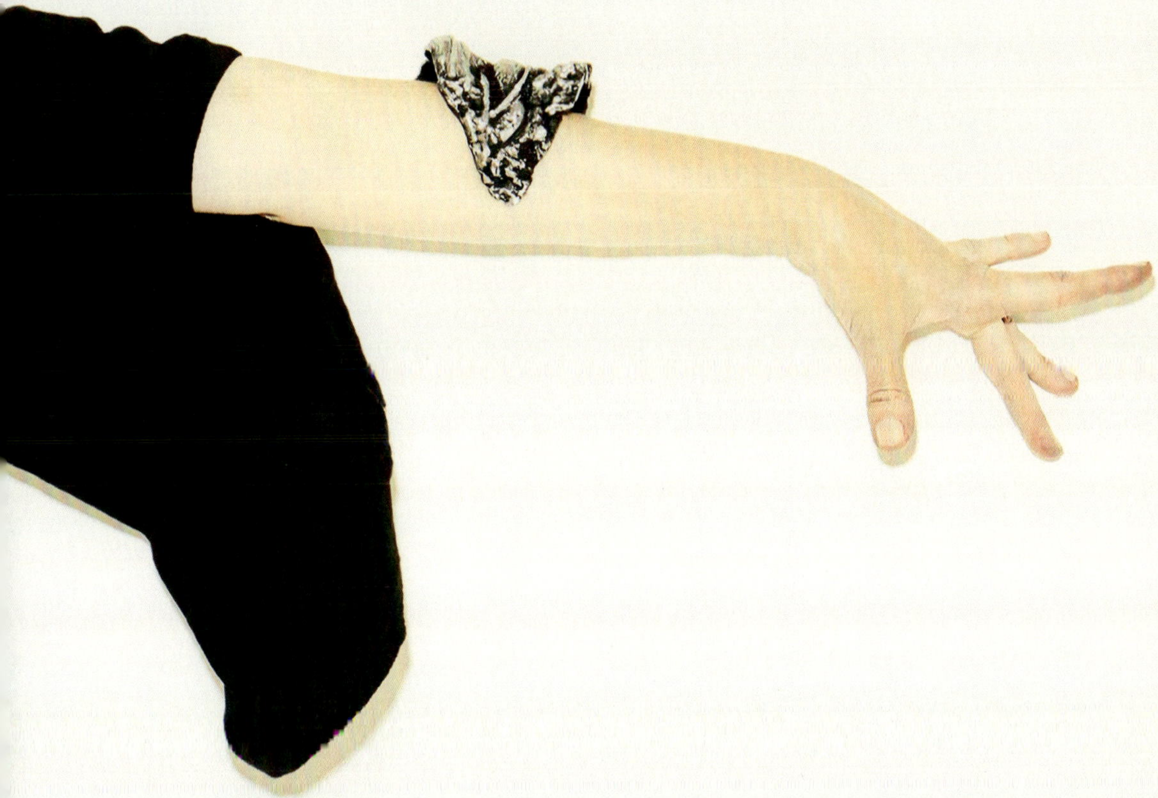

Hip Piece, 2016
Aluminum

Shoulder Piece, 2016
Aluminum

Arm Piece, 2016
Aluminum

Shoulder Piece, 2016
Aluminum

Hip Piece, 2016
Aluminum

Arm Piece, 2016
Aluminum

Matthew Day Jackson

Seeing Eye Ring, 2016 (left)
14 kt gold and sterling silver

Vanitas I, 2013 (right)
18 kt yellow gold and diamond

Vanitas I, 2013
Ring: 18 kt yellow gold and diamond. Skull top: 22 kt yellow gold plated silver
Skull bottom: 18 kt yellow gold plated silver
Base: electroformed rhodium plated silver and carved wood

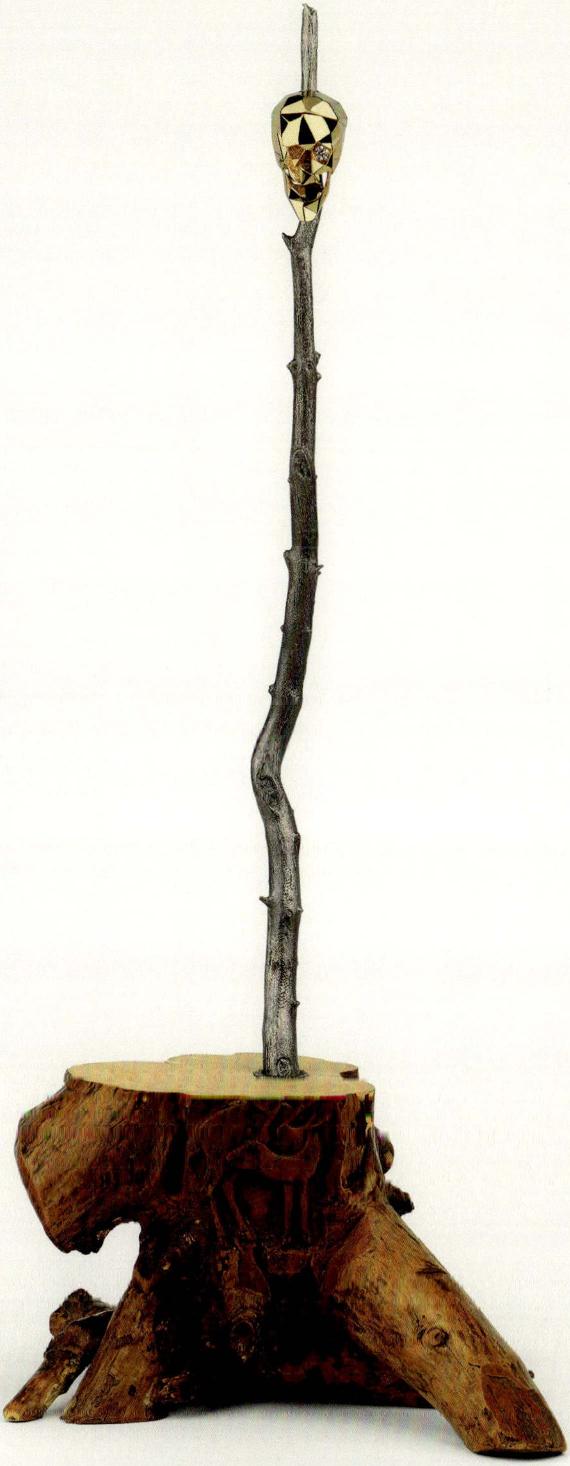

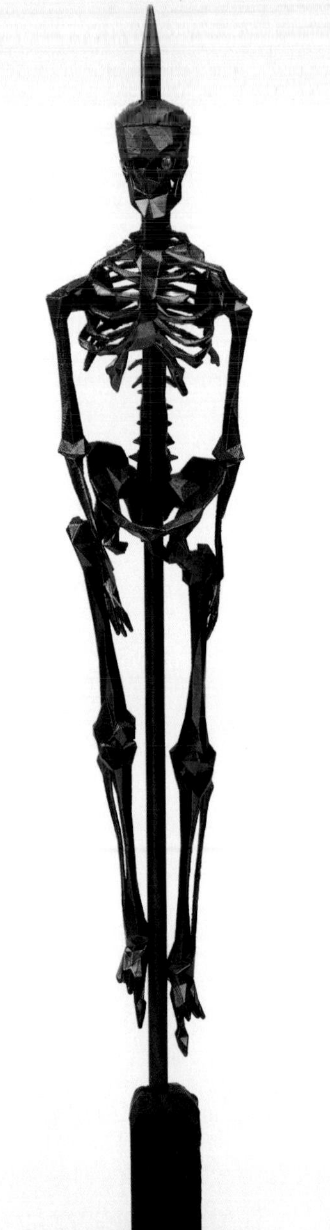

Vanitas II, 2016
Ring: electroformed blackened silver and sapphire
Skeleton: electroformed blackened silver
Base: bronze

Bharti Kher

Warrior Bracelet, 2017
22 kt yellow gold plated silver

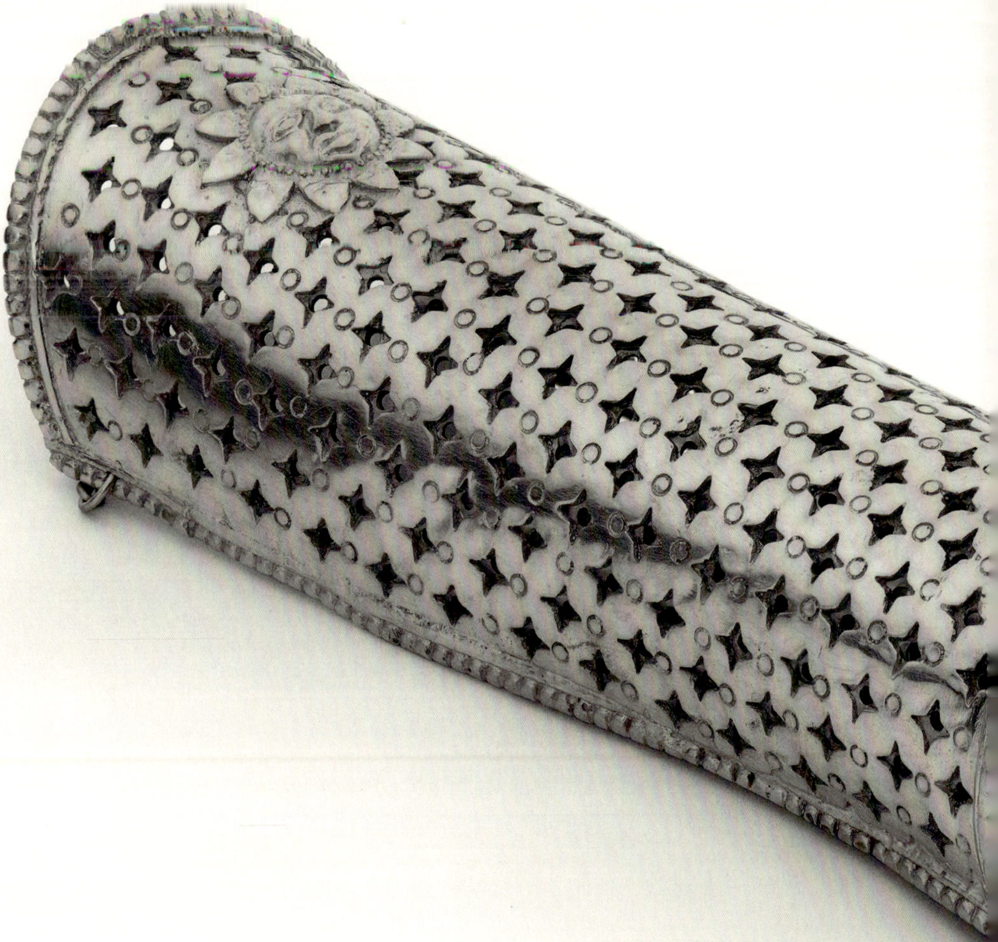

*The piece is a talisman protector.
It's like my work that
carries in it the material and the
power of another. Like a skin
the shaman carries. Wear it to
work and keep it in your bedroom
for when you need to call into
being your warrior.*

Bharti Kher

Previous spread: Warrior Bracelet, 2016
Rhodium plated silver

Warrior Bracelet, 2016
Rose gold plated silver

Nate Lowman

Iron Boom I, 2011
Steel, champagne and brown diamonds

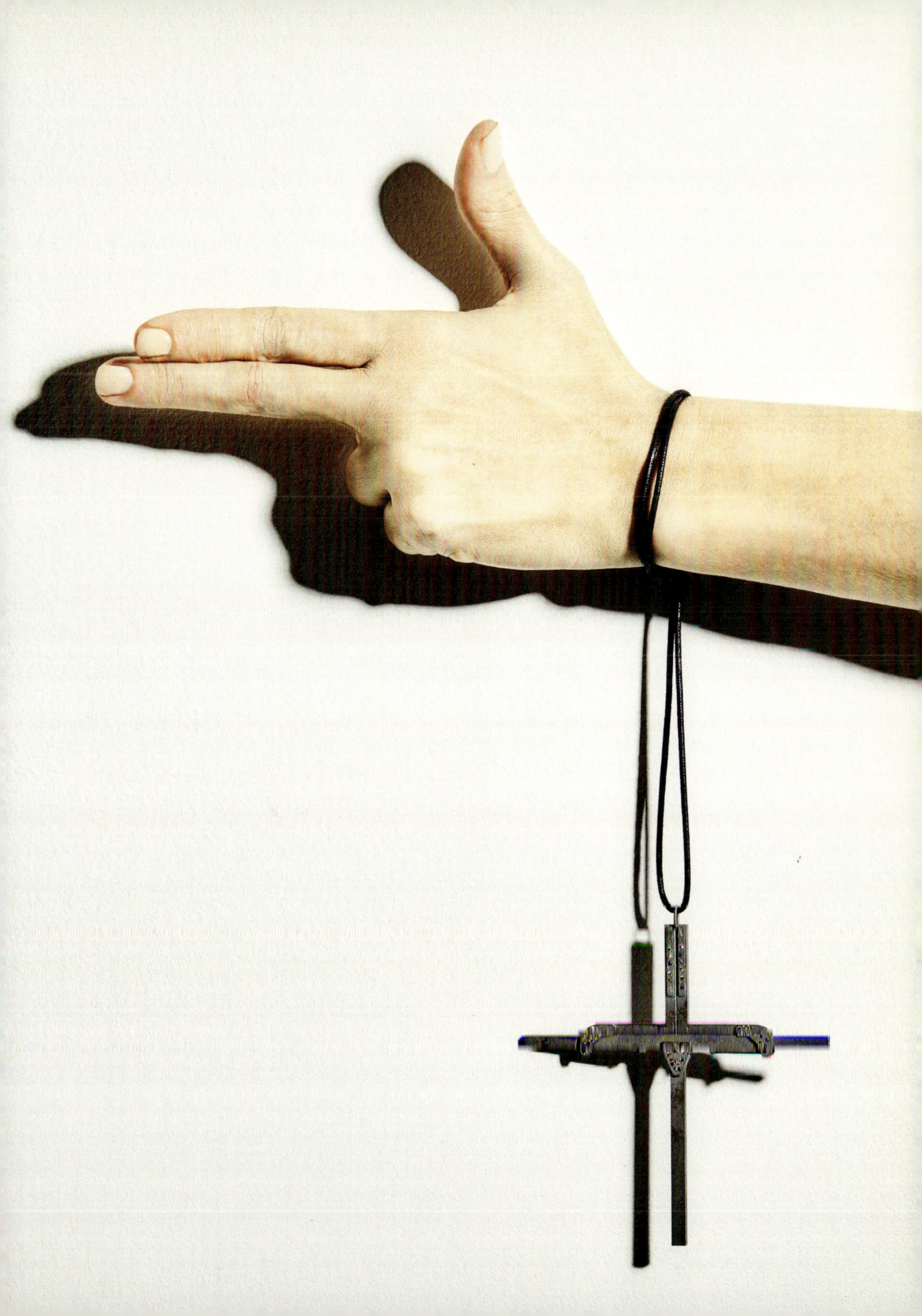

Iron Boom I, 2011
Steel, champagne and brown diamonds

Iron Boom III, 2011 (detail)
Steel, champagne and brown diamonds

Paul McCarthy

Butt Plug Necklace, 2014 (left)
Rose gold plated 18 kt yellow gold

Butt Plug Necklace, 2013 (middle)
18 kt yellow gold

Butt Plug Necklace, 2011 (right)
Silver

Butt Plug Necklace, 2013
18 kt yellow gold

Butt Plug Necklace, 2013
18 kt yellow gold

Butt Plug Necklace, 2014
Rose gold plated 18 kt yellow gold

Butt Plug Necklace, 2011
Silver

Caro Niederer

Charm Bracelet I, 2009 (right)
Bracelet: 22 kt yellow gold plated silver
7 charms: photographs, glass

Charm Bracelet III, 2009 (left)
Bracelet: 22 kt yellow gold plated silver
7 charms: photographs, glass

Charm Bracelet I, 2009
Bracelet: 22 kt yellow gold plated silver
7 charms: photographs, glass

Charm Bracelet II, 2009
Bracelet: 22 kt yellow gold plated silver
7 charms: photographs, glass

Charm Bracelet I, 2009 (back)
Bracelet: 22 kt yellow gold plated silver
7 charms: photographs, glass

Charm Bracelet III, 2009 (front)
Bracelet: 22 kt yellow gold plated silver
7 charms: photographs, glass

Michele Oka Doner

Nekton, 2016
Bronze necklace set with diamonds

Plankton, 2016
Bronze bracelet set with diamonds

My jewelry is a condensation of the ideas invested in larger works, a compression like perfume, reducing the meadow into a few drops. The essence is captured and embodied on a different scale, a human measure.

Michele Oka Doner

Previous spread: Nekton, 2016
Bronze necklace set with diamonds

Plankton, 2016
Bronze bracelet set with diamonds

Pipilotti Rist

Jewellery for Wintertimes, 2016
Polycarbonate and electrical cable